SAYINGS AND UTTERANCES

Swami Vivekananda

JOLLYJOY

ABOUT THE AUTHOR

Swami Vivekananda, born Narendranath Datta on January 12, 1863, in Kolkata, India, was a key figure in introducing Hindu philosophy to the Western world. A disciple of the mystic Ramakrishna, Vivekananda played a pivotal role in the revival of Hinduism and the promotion of Vedanta.

He gained international fame at the Parliament of Religions in Chicago in 1893, where his powerful speech emphasized the unity of all religions and the importance of tolerance. His teachings focused on the idea of self-realization, the potential of every individual, and the necessity of combining spirituality with practical action for societal betterment.

Vivekananda founded the Ramakrishna Mission in 1897, promoting social service, education, and spiritual development. His writings, including "Raja Yoga" and "Karma Yoga," delve into the practical applications of yoga and the importance of selfless action.

A visionary thinker, he inspired generations with his ideas on spirituality, nationalism, and human potential, leaving a lasting legacy that continues to influence millions worldwide. Swami Vivekananda passed away on January 19, 1902, but his teachings remain relevant, advocating for the harmony of science and spirituality, and encouraging individuals to pursue their highest potential.

Sayings And Utterances

by Swami Vivekananda

Published by Jollyjoy Books Pvt Ltd.

JOLLYJOY
BOOKS

4771/23, Bharat Ram Road, Daryaganj,

New Delhi-110002

E-mail: Contact@jollyjoybooks.com

ISBN: 978-93-6849-097-5

Cover, Typesetting, and Book Design by JollyJoy Books

CONTENTS

Part- I

SAYINGS AND UTTERANCES

1. Man is born to conquer nature and not to follow it.

2. When you think you are a body, are apart from the universe; when you think; you are a soul, you are a spark from the great Eternal Fire; when you think you are the Âtman (Self), you are All.

3. The will is not free — it is a phenomenon bound by cause and effect — but there is something behind the will which is free.

4. Strength is in goodness, in purity.

5. The universe is — objectified God.

6. You cannot believe in God until you believe in yourself.

7. The root of evil is in the illusion that we are bodies. This, if any, is the original sin.

8. One party says thought is caused by matter, and the other says matter is caused by thought. Both statements are wrong; matter and thought are coexistent. There is a third something of which both matter and thought are products.

9. As particles of matter combine in space, so mind-waves combine in time.

10. To define God is — grinding the already ground; for He is the only being we know.

11. Religion is the idea which is raising the brute unto man, and man unto God.

12. External nature is only internal nature writ large.

13. The motive is the measure of your work. What motive can be higher than that you are God, and that the lowest man is also God?

14. The observer in the psychic world needs to be very strong and scientifically trained.

15. To believe that mind is all, that thought is all is only a higher materialism.

16. This world is the great gymnasium where we come to make ourselves strong.

17. You cannot teach a child any more than you can grow a plant. All you can do is on the negative side — you can only help. It is a manifestation from within; it develops its own nature — you can only take away obstructions.

18. As soon as you make a sect, you protest against universal brotherhood. Those who really feel universal brotherhood do not talk much, but their very actions speak aloud.

19. Truth can be stated in a thousand different ways, yet each one can be true.

20. You have to grow from inside out. None can teach you, none can make you spiritual. There is no other teacher but your own soul.

21. If in an infinite chain a few links can be explained, by the same method all can be explained.

22. That man has reached immortality who is disturbed by nothing material.

23. Everything can be sacrificed for truth, but truth cannot be

sacrificed for anything.

24. The search for truth is the expression of strength — not the groping of a weak, blind man.

25. God has become man; man will become God again.

26. It is child's talk that a man dies and goes to heaven. We never come nor go. We are where we are. All the souls that have been, are, and will be, are on one geometrical point.

27. He whose book of the heart has been opened needs no other books. Their only value is to create desire in us. They are merely the experiences of others.

28. Have charity towards all beings. Pity those who are in distress. Love all creatures. Do not be jealous of anyone. Look not to the faults of others.

29. Man never dies, nor is he ever born; bodies die, but he never dies.

30. No one is born into a religion, but each one is born for a religion.

31. There is really but one Self in the universe, all else is but Its manifestations.

32. All the worshippers are divided into the common masses and the brave few.

33. If it is impossible to attain perfection here and now, there is no proof that we can attain perfection in any other life.

34. If I know one lump of clay perfectly, I know all the clay there is. This is the knowledge of principles, but their adaptations are various. When you know yourself you know all.

35. Personally I take as much of the Vedas as agrees with reason. Parts of the Vedas are apparently contradictory. They are not considered as inspired in the Western sense of the word, but as the sum total of the knowledge of God, omniscience. This knowledge comes out at the beginning of a cycle and manifests itself; and when

the cycle ends, it goes down into minute form. When the cycle is projected again, that knowledge is projected again with it. So far the theory is all right. But that only these books which are called the Vedas are His knowledge is mere sophistry. Manu says in one pace that that part of the Vedas which agrees with reason is the Vedas and nothing else. Many of our philosophers have taken this view.

36. Of all the scriptures of the world it is the Vedas alone that declare that even the study of the Vedas is secondary. The real study is "that by which we realise the Unchangeable". And that is neither reading, for believing, nor reasoning, but superconscious perception, or Samâdhi.

37. We have been low animals once. We think they are something different from us. I hear, Western people say, "The world was created for us." If tigers could write books, they would say, man was created for them and that man is a most sinful animal, because he does not allow him (the tiger) to catch him easily. The worm that crawls under your feet today is a God to be.

38. "I should very much like our women to have your intellectuality, but not if it must be at the cost of purity", said Swami Vivekananda in New York. "I admire you for all that you know, but I dislike the way that you cover what is bad with roses and call it good. Intellectuality is not the highest good. Morality and spirituality are the things for which we strive. Our women are not so learned, but they are more pure.

"To all women every man save her husband should be as her son. To all men every woman save his own wife should be as his mother. When I look about me and see what you call gallantry, my soul is filled with disgust. Not until you learn to ignore the question of sex and to meet on a ground of common humanity will your women really develop. Until then they are playthings, nothing more. All this is the cause of divorce. Your men bow low and offer a chair, but in another breath they offer compliments. They say, 'Oh, madam, how beautiful are your eyes!' What right have they to do this? How dare a man venture so far, and how can you women permit it? Such things develop the less noble side of humanity. They do not tend to nobler ideals.

"We should not think that we are men and women. but only that we are human beings, born to cherish and to help one another. No sooner are a young man and a young woman left alone than he pays compliments to her, and perhaps before he takes a wife, he has courted two hundred women. Bah! If I belonged to the marrying set, I could find a woman to love without all that!

"When I was in India and saw these things from the outside, I was told it was all right, it was mere pleasantry and I believed it. But I have travelled since then, and I know it is not right. It is wrong, only you of the West shut your eyes and call it good. The trouble with the nations of the West is that they are young, foolish, fickle, and wealthy. What mischief can come of one of these qualities; but when all three, all four, are combined beware!"

But severe as the Swami was upon all, Boston received the hardest blow:

"Of all, Boston is the worst. There the women are all faddists, all fickle, merely bent on following something new and strange."

39. "Where is the spirituality one would expect in a country", he said in America, "that is so boastful of its civilisation?"

40. "Here" and "hereafter" are words to frighten children. It is all "here". To live and move in God even here, even in this body, all self should go out, all superstition should be banished. Such persons live in India. Where are such in this country (America)? Your preachers speak against dreamers. The people of this country would be better off if there were more dreamers. There is a good deal of difference between dreaming and the brag of the nineteenth century. The whole world is full of God and not of sin. Let us help one another, let us love one another.

41. Let me die a true Sannyâsin as my Master did, heedless of money, of women, and of fame! And of these the most insidious is the love of fame!

42. I have never spoken of revenge, I have always spoken of

strength. Do we dream of revenging ourselves on this drop of sea-spray? But it is a great thing to a mosquito!

43. "This is a great land," said Swamiji on one occasion in America, "but I would not like to live here. Americans think too much of money. They give it preference over anything else. Your people have much to learn. When your nation is as old as ours, you will be wiser."

44. It may be that I shall find it good to get outside of my body — to cast it off like a disused garment. But I shall not cease to work! I shall inspire men everywhere, until the world shall know that it is one with God.

45. All that I am, all that the world itself will some day be, is owing to my Master, Shri Ramakrishna, who incarnated and experienced and taught this wonderful unity which underlies everything, having discovered it alike in Hinduism, in Islam, and in Christianity.

46. Give the organ of taste a free rein, and the other organs will also run on unbridled.

47. Jnâna, Bhakti, Yoga and Karma — these are the four paths which lead to salvation. One must follow the path for which one is best suited; but in this age special stress should be laid on Karma-Yoga.

48. Religion is not a thing of imagination but of direct perception. He who has seen even a single spirit is greater than many a book-learned Pandit.

49. Once Swamiji was praising someone very much; at this, one sitting near by said to him, "But he does not believe in you." Hearing this, Swamiji at once replied: "Is there any legal affidavit that he should have to do so? He is doing good work, and so he is worthy of praise."

50. In the domain of true religion, book-learning has no right to enter.

51. The downfall of a religious sect begins from the day that the worship of the rich enters into it.

52. If you want to do anything evil, do it before the eyes of your superiors.

53. By the grace of the Guru, a disciple becomes a Pandit (scholar) even without reading books.

54. There is no sin nor virtue: there is only ignorance. By realisation of non- duality this ignorance is dispelled.

55. Religious movements come in groups. Each one of them tries to rear itself above the rest. But as a rule only one of them really grows in strength, and this, in the long run, swallows up all the contemporary movements.

56. When Swamiji was at Ramnad, he said in the course of a conversation that Shri Râma was the Paramâtman and that Sitâ was the Jivâtman, and each man's or woman's body was the Lanka (Ceylon). The Jivatman which was enclosed in the body, or captured in the island of Lankâ, always desired to be in affinity with the Paramatman, or Shri Rama. But the Râkshasas would not allow it, and Rakshasas represented certain traits of character. For instance, Vibhishana represented Sattva Guna; Râvana, Rajas; and Kumbhakarna, Tamas. Sattva Guna means goodness; Rajas means lust and passions, and Tamas darkness, stupor, avarice, malice, and its concomitants. These Gunas keep back Sita, or Jivatman, which is in the body, or Lanka, from joining Paramatman, or Rama. Sita, thus imprisoned and trying to unite with her Lord, receives a visit from Hanumân, the Guru or divine teacher, who shows her the Lord's ring, which is Brahma-Jnâna, the supreme wisdom that destroys all illusions; and thus Sita finds the way to be at one with Shri Rama, or, in other words, the Jivatman finds itself one with the Paramatman.

57. A true Christian is a true Hindu, and a true Hindu is a true Christian.

58. All healthy social changes are the manifestations of the spiritual forces working within, and if these are strong and well adjusted, society will arrange itself accordingly. Each individual has to work out his own salvation; there is no other way, and so also with nations. Again, the great institutions of every nation are the

conditions of its very existence and cannot be transformed by the mould of any other race. Until higher institutions have been evolved, any attempt to break the old ones will be disastrous. Growth is always gradual.

It is very easy to point out the defects of institutions, all being more or less imperfect, but he is the real benefactor of humanity who helps the individual to overcome his imperfections under whatever institutions he may live. The individuals being raised, the nation and its institutions are bound to rise. Bad customs and laws are ignored by the virtuous, and unwritten but mightier laws of love, sympathy, and integrity take their place. Happy is the nation which can rise to the necessity of but few law books, and needs no longer to bother its head about this or that institution. Good men rise beyond all laws, and will help their fellows to rise under whatever conditions they live.

The salvation of India, therefore, depends on the strength of the individual, and the realisation by each man of the divinity within.

59. Spirituality can never be attained until materiality is gone.

60. The first discourse in the Gita can be taken allegorically.

61. "Swami, you have no idea of time", remarked an impatient American devotee, afraid of missing a steamer. "No," retorted Swamiji calmly, "you live in time; we live in eternity!"

62. We are always letting sentiment usurp the place of duty and flatter ourselves that we are acting in response to true love.

63. We must get beyond emotionalism if we want the power to renounce. Emotion belongs to the animals. They are creatures of emotion entirely.

64. It is not sacrifice of a high order to die for one's young. The animals do that, and just as readily as any human mother ever did. It is no sign of real love to do that; it is merely blind emotion.

65. We are for ever trying to make our weakness look like strength, our sentiment like love, our cowardice like courage, and so

on.

66. Say to your soul in regard to vanities, weakness, etc., "This does not befit thee. This does not befit thee."

67. Never loved a husband the wife for the wife's sake or the wife the husband for the husband's sake. It is God in the wife the husband loves, and God in the husband the wife loves. It is God in every one that draws us to the one we love, God in everything and in everybody that makes us love. God is the only love.

68. Oh, if only you knew yourselves! You are souls; you are Gods. If ever I feel like blaspheming, it; is when I call you man.

69. In everyone is God, the Atman; all else is but dream, an illusion.

70. If I do not find bliss in the life of the Spirit, shall, I seek satisfaction in the life of the senses? If I cannot get nectar; shall I fall back upon ditch water? The bird called Châtaka drinks from the clouds only, ever calling as it soars, "Pure water! Pure water!" And no storms or tempests make it falter on wing or descend to drink from the earth.

71. Any sect that may help you to realise God is welcome. Religion is the realising of God.

72. An atheist can be charitable but not religious. But the religious man must be charitable.

73. Everyone makes shipwreck on the rock of would-be Guruism, except those souls that were born to be Gurus.

74. Man is a compound of animality, humanity, and divinity.

75. The term "social progress" has as much meaning as "hot ice" or "dark light". There is no such thing, ultimately, as "social progress"!

76. Things are not bettered, but we are bettered, by making changes in them.

77. Let me help my fellow men; that is all I seek.

78. "No", said the Swami, very softly, in answer to a question in New York, "I do not believe in the occult. If a thing be unreal, it is not. What is unreal does not exist. Strange things are natural phenomena. I know them to be matters of science. Then they are not occult to me. I do not believe in occult societies. They do no good, and can never do good."

79. There are four general types of men — the rational, the emotional, the mystical, and the worker. For each of these we must provide suitable forms of worship. There comes the rational man, who says, "I care not for this form of worship. Give me the philosophical, the rational — that I can appreciate." So for the rational man is the rational philosophic worship.

There comes the worker. He says, "I care not for the worship of the philosopher. Give me work to do for my fellow men." So for him is provided work as the path of worship. As for the mystical and the emotional, we have their respective modes of devotion. All these men have, in religion, the elements of their faith.

80. I stand for truth. Truth will never ally itself with falsehood. Even if all the world should be against me, Truth must prevail in the end.

81. Wherever you see the most humanitarian ideas fall into the hands of the multitude, the first result you notice is degradation. It is learning and intellect that help to keep things safe. It is the cultured among a community that are the real custodians of religion and philosophy in their purest form. It is that form which serves as the index for the intellectual and social condition of a community.

82. "I do not come", said Swamiji on one occasion in America, "to convert you to a new belief. I want you to keep your own belief; I want to make the Methodist a better Methodist; the Presbyterian a better Presbyterian; the Unitarian a better Unitarian. I want to teach you to live the truth, to reveal the light within your own soul."

83. Happiness presents itself before man, wearing the crown of sorrow on its head. He who welcomes it must also welcome sorrow.

84. He is free, he is great, who turns his back upon the world,

who has renounced everything, who has controlled his passion, and who thirsts for peace. One may gain political and social independence, but if one is a slave to his passions and desires, one cannot feel the pure joy of real freedom.

85. Doing good to others is virtue (Dharma); injuring others is sin. Strength and manliness are virtue; weakness and cowardice are sin. Independence is virtue; dependence is sin. Loving others is virtue; hating others is sin. Faith in God and in one's own Self is virtue; doubt is sin. Knowledge of oneness is virtue; seeing diversity is sin. The different scriptures only show the means of attaining virtue.

86. When, by reasoning, Truth is comprehended by the intellect, then it is realised in the heart, the fountainhead of feeling. Thus the head and the heart become illumined at the same moment; and then only, as says the Upanishad, "The knot of the heart is rent asunder, and all doubts cease" (Mundaka Upanishad, II.ii.8).

When in ancient times this knowledge (Jnâna) and this feeling (Bhâva) thus blossomed forth simultaneously in the heart of the Rishi, then the Highest Truth became poetic, and then the Vedas and other scriptures were composed. It is for this reason that one finds, in studying them, that the two parallel lines of Bhava and Jnana have at last met, as it were, in the plane of the Vedas and become combined and inseparable.

87. The scriptures of different religions point out different means to attain the ideals of universal love, freedom, manliness, and selfless benevolence. Every religious sect is generally at variance as to its idea of what is virtue and what is vice, and fights with others over the means of attaining virtue and eschewing vice, instead of aiming at realising the end. Every means is helpful more or less, and the Gita (XVIII.48) says, "Every undertaking is attended with defects as fire with smoke"; so the means will no doubt appear more or less defective. But as we are to attain the highest virtue through the means laid dozen in our respective scriptures, we should try our best to follow them. Moreover, they should be tempered with reason and discrimination. Thus, as we progress, the riddle of virtue and

vice will be solved by itself.

88. How many in our country truly understand the Shastras nowadays? They have only learnt such words as Brahman, Maya, Prakriti, and so on, and confuse their heads with them. Setting aside the real meaning and purpose of the Shastras, they fight over the words only. If the Shastras cannot help all men in all conditions at all times, of what use, then, are such Shastras? If the Shastras show the way to the Sannyasins only and not to the householders, then what need has a householder for such one-sided Shastras? If the Shastras can only help men when they give up all work and retire into the forests, and cannot show the way of lighting the lamp of hope in the hearts of men of the workaday world — in the midst of their daily toil, disease, misery, and poverty, in the despondency of the penitent, in the self-reproach of the downtrodden, in the terror of the battlefield, in lust, anger and pleasure, in the joy of victory, in the darkness of defeat, and finally, in the dreaded night of death — then weak humanity has no need of such Shastras, and such Shastras will be no Shastras at all!

89. Through Bhoga (enjoyment) Yoga will come in time. But alas, such is the lot of my countrymen that, not to speak of possessing yoga, they cannot even have a little Bhoga! Suffering all sorts of indignities they can with the utmost difficulty only meet the barest needs of the body — and even that everyone cannot do! It is strange that such a state of affairs does not disturb our sleep and rouse us to our immediate duties.

90. Agitate ever so much for your rights and privileges, but remember that so long as we do not truly elevate ourselves by rousing intensely the feeling of self-respect in the nation, so long our hope of gaining rights and privileges is like the day-dream of Alnascar.

91. When a genius of a man with some special great power is born, all the best and the most creative faculties of his whole heredity are drawn towards the making up of his personality and squeezed dry, as it were. It is for this reason that we find that all those who are subsequently born in such a family are either idiots or men of very ordinary calibre, and that in time such a family in many cases

becomes extinct.

92. If you cannot attain salvation in this life, what proof is there that you can attain it in the life or lives to come?

93. While visiting the Taj at Agra he remarked: "If you squeeze a bit of this marble, it will drip drops of royal love and its sorrow." Further he observed, "It takes really six months to study a square inch of its interior works of beauty."

94. When the real history of India will be unearthed, it will be proved that, as in matters of religion, so in fine arts, India is the primal Guru of the whole world.

95. Speaking of architecture he said: "People say Calcutta is a city of palaces, but the houses look much like so many boxes placed one upon the other! They convey no idea whatever. In Rajputana you can still find much pure Hindu architecture. If you look at a Dharmashala, you will feel as if it calls you with open arms to take shelter within and partake of its unqualified hospitableness. If you look at a temple, you are sure to find a Divine Presence in and about it. If you look about a rural cottage, you will at once be able to comprehend the special meanings of its different portions, and that the whole structure bears evidence to the predominant nature and ideal of the owner thereof. This sort of expressive architecture I have seen nowhere else except in Italy."

Part- II

SAYINGS AND UTTERANCES

1. "Did Buddha teach that the many was real and the ego unreal, while orthodox Hinduism regards the One as the real, and the many as unreal?" the Swami was asked. "Yes", answered the Swami. "And what Ramakrishna Paramahamsa and I have added to this is, that the Many and the One are the same Reality, perceived by the same mind at different times and in different attitudes."

2. "Remember!" he said once to a disciple, "Remember! the message of India is always 'Not the soul for nature, but nature for the soul!'"

3. "What the world wants today is twenty men and women who can dare to stand in the street yonder, and say that they possess nothing but God. Who will go? Why should one fear? If this is true, what else could matter? If it is not true, what do our lives matter!"

4. "Oh, how calm would be the work of one who really understood the divinity of man! For such, there is nothing to do, save to open men's eyes. All the rest does itself."

5. "He (Shri Ramakrishna) was contented simply to live that great life and to leave it to others to find the explanation!"

6. "Plans! Plans!" Swami Vivekananda explained in indignation,

when one of his disciples had offered him some piece of worldly wisdom. "That is why . . . Western people can never create a religion! If any of you ever did, it was only a few Catholic saints who had no plans. Religion was never preached by planners!"

7. "Social life in the West is like a peal of laughter; but underneath, it is a wail. It ends in a sob. The fun and frivolity are all on the surface: really it is full of tragic intensity. Now here, it is sad and gloomy on the outside, but underneath are carelessness and merriment.

"We have a theory that the universe is God's manifestation of Himself just for fun, that the Incarnations came and lived here 'just for fun'. Play, it was all play. Why was Christ crucified? It was mere play. And so of life. Just play with the Lord. Say, "It is all play, it is all play". Do you do anything?"

8. "I am persuaded that a leader is not made in one life. He has to be born for it. For the difficulty is not in organisation and making plans; the test, the real test, of the leader, lies in holding widely different people together along the line of their common sympathies. And this can only be done unconsciously, never by trying."

9. In explanation of Plato's doctrine of Ideas, Swamiji said, "And so you see, all this is but a feeble manifestation of the great ideas, which alone, are real and perfect. Somewhere is an ideal for you, and here is an attempt to manifest it! The attempt falls short still in many ways. Still, go on! You will interpret the ideal some day."

10. Answering the remark of a disciple who felt that it would be better for her to come back to this life again and again and help the causes that were of interest to her instead of striving for personal salvation with a deep longing to get out of life, the Swami retorted quickly: "That's because you cannot overcome the idea of progress. But things do not grow better. They remain as they are; and we grow better by the changes we make in them."

11. It was in Almora that a certain elderly man, with a face full of amiable weakness, came and put him a question about Karma.

What were they to do, he asked, whose Karma it was to see the strong oppress the weak? The Swami turned on him in surprised indignation. "Why, thrash the strong, of course!" he said, "You forget your own part in this Karma: Yours is always the right to rebel!"

12. "Ought one to seek an opportunity of death in defense of right, or ought one to take the lesson of the Gitâ and learn never to react?" the Swami was asked. "I am for no reaction", said the Swami, speaking slowly and with a long pause. Then he added " — for Sannyâsins. Self-defense for the householder!"

13. "It is a mistake to hold that with all men pleasure is the motive. Quite as many are born to seek after pain. Let us worship the Terror for Its own sake."

14. "Ramakrishna Paramahamsa was the only man who ever had the courage to say that we must speak to all men in their own language!"

15. "How I used to hate Kâli!" he said, referring to his own days of doubts in accepting the Kali ideal, "And all Her ways! That was the ground of my six years' fight — that I would not accept Her. But I had to accept Her at last! Ramakrishna Paramahamsa dedicated me to Her, and now I believe that She guides me in everything I do, and does with me what She will Yet I fought so long! I loved him, you see, and that was what held me. I saw his marvellous purity. . . . I felt his wonderful love. . . . His greatness had not dawned on me then. All that came afterwards when I had given in. At that time I thought him a brain-sick baby, always seeing visions and the rest. I hated it. And then I, too, had to accept Her!

"No, the thing that made me do it is a secret that will die with me. I had great misfortunes at the time. . . . It was an opportunity. . . . She made a slave of me.

Those were the very words: 'a slave of you'. And Ramakrishna Paramahamsa made me over to Her. . . . Strange! He lived only two years after doing that, and most of the time he was suffering. Not more than six months did he keep his own health and brightness.

"Guru Nanak was like that, you know, looking for the one disciple to whom he would give his power. And he passed over all his own family — his children were as nothing to him — till he came upon the boy to whom he gave it; and then he could die.

"The future, you say, will call Ramakrishna Paramahamsa an Incarnation of Kali? Yes, I think there's no doubt that She worked up the body of Ramakrishna for Her own ends.

"You see, I cannot but believe that there is somewhere a great Power that thinks of Herself as feminine, and called Kali and Mother. . . . And I believe in Brahman too. . . . But is it not always like that? Is it not the multitude of cells in the body that make up the personality, the many brain-centres, not the one, that produce consciousness? . . . Unity in complexity! Just so! And why should it be different with Brahman? It is Brahman. It is the One. And yet — and yet — it is the gods too!"

16. "The older I grow, the more everything seems to me to lie in manliness. This is my new gospel."

17. Referring to some European reference to cannibalism, as if it were a normal part of life in some societies, the Swami remarked, "That is not true! No nation ever ate human flesh, save as a religious sacrifice, or in war, out of revenge. Don't you see? That's not the way of gregarious animals! It would cut at the root of social life!"

18. "Sex-love and creation! These are at the root of most religions. And these in India are called Vaishnavism, and in the West Christianity. How few have dared to worship Death or Kali! Let us worship Death! Let us embrace the Terrible, because it is terrible, not asking that it be toned down. Let us take misery for misery's own sake!"

19. "The three cycles of Buddhism were five hundred years of the Law, five hundred years of images, and five hundred years of Tantras. You must not imagine that there was ever a religion in India called Buddhism with temples and priests of its own order!

Nothing of the sort. It was always within Hinduism. Only at one time the influence of Buddha was paramount, and this made the nation monastic."

20. "The conservative's whole ideal is submission. Your ideal is struggle.

Consequently it is we who enjoy the life, and never you! You are always striving to change yours to something better; and before a millionth part of the change is carried out, you die. The Western ideal is to be doing; the Eastern to be suffering. The perfect life would be a wonderful harmony doing and suffering. But that can never be.

"In our system it is accepted that a man cannot have all he desires. Life is subjected to many restraints. This is ugly, yet it brings out points of light and strength. Our liberals see only the ugliness and try to throw it off. But they substitute something quite as bad; and the new custom takes as long as the old for us to work to its centres of strength.

"Will is not strengthened by change. It is weakened and enslaved by it. But we must be always absorbing. Will grows stronger by absorption. And consciously or unconsciously, will is the one thing in the world that we admire. Suttee is great in the eyes of the whole world, because of the will that it manifests.

"It is selfishness that we must seek to eliminate. I find that whenever I have made a mistake in my life, it has always been because self entered into the calculation. Where self has not been involved, my judgment has gone straight to the mark.

"Without self, there would have been no religious system. If man had not wanted anything for himself, do you think he would have had all this praying and worship? Why! he would never have thought of God at all, except perhaps for a little praise now and then, at the sight of a beautiful landscape or something. And that is the only attitude there ought to be. All praise and thanks. If only we were rid of self!

"You are quite wrong when you think that fighting is a sign of growth. It is not so at all. Absorption is the sign. Hinduism is a very genius of absorption. We have never cared for fighting. Of course we could strike a blow now and then, in defense of our homes! That was right. But we never cared for fighting for its own sake. Every one had to learn that. So let these races of newcomers whirl on! They'll all be taken into Hinduism in the end!"

21. "The totality of all souls, not the human alone, is the Personal God. The will of the Totality nothing can resist. It is what we know as law. And this is what we mean by Shiva and Kali and so on."

22. "Worship the Terrible! Worship Death! All else is vain. All struggle is vain. That is the last lesson. Yet this is not the coward's love of death, not the love of the weak or the suicide. It is the welcome of the strong man who has sounded everything to its depths and knows that there is no alternative."

23. "I disagree with all those who are giving their superstitions back to my people. Like the Egyptologist's interest in Egypt, it is easy to feel an interest in India that is purely selfish. One may desire to see again the India of one's books, one's studies, one's dreams. My hope is to see again the strong points of that India, reinforced by the strong points of this age, only in a natural way. The new stage of things must be a growth from within.

"So I preach only the Upanishads. If you look, you will find that I have never quoted anything but the Upanishads. And of the Upanishads, it is only that One idea, strength. The quintessence of the Vedas and Vedanta and all lies in that one word. Buddha's teaching was non-resistance, or non-injury. But I think this is a better way of teaching the same thing. For behind that non-injury lay a dreadful weakness. It is weakness that conceives the idea of resistance. I do not think of punishing or escaping from a drop of sea-spray. It is nothing to me. Yet to the mosquito it would be serious. Now I would make all injury like that. Strength and fearlessness. My own ideal is that saint whom they killed in the Mutiny and who broke his silence, when stabbed to the heart, to say, 'And thou also art He!'

"But you may ask, 'What is the place of Ramakrishna in this scheme?'

"He is the method, that wonderful unconscious method! He did not understand himself. He knew nothing of England or the English, save that they were queer folk from over the sea. But he lived that great life: and I read the meaning. Never a word of condemnation for any! Once I had been attacking one of our sects of diabolists. I had been raving on for three hours, and he had listened quietly. 'Well, well!' said the old man as I finished, 'perhaps every house may have a backdoor. Who knows?'

"Hitherto the great fault of our Indian religion has lain in its knowing only two words: renunciation and Mukti. Only Mukti here! Nothing for the householder! "But these are the very people whom I want to help. For are not all souls of the same quality? Is not the goal of all the same?

"And so strength must come to the nation through education."

24. The Puranas, the Swami considered, to be the effort of Hinduism to bring lofty ideas to the door of the masses. There had been only one mind in India that had foreseen this need, that of Krishna, probably the greatest man who ever lived.

The Swami said, "Thus is created a religion that ends in the worship of Vishnu, as the preservation and enjoyment of life, leading to the realisation of God.

Our last movement, Chaitanyaism, you remember, was for enjoyment. At the same time Jainism represents the other extreme, the slow destruction of the body by self-torture. Hence Buddhism, you see, is reformed Jainism; and this is the real meaning of Buddha's leaving the company of the five ascetics. In India, in every age, there is a cycle of sects which represents every gradation of physical practice, from the extreme of self-torture to the extreme of excess. And during the same period will always be developed a metaphysical cycle, which represents the realisation of God as taking place by every gradation of means, from that of using the senses as an instrument to that of the annihilation of the senses. Thus Hinduism always consists, as it were, of two counter- spirals, completing each other, round a single axis.

"'Yes!' Vaishnavism says, 'it is all right — this tremendous love for father, for mother, for brother, husband, or child! It is all right, if only you will think that Krishna is the child, and when you give him food, that you are feeding Krishna!' This was the cry of Chaitanya, 'Worship God through the senses', as against the Vedantic cry, 'Control the senses! suppress the senses!'

"I see that India is a young and living organism. Europe is young and living. Neither has arrived at such a stage of development that we can safely criticise its institutions. They are two great experiments, neither of which is yet complete. In India we have social communism, with the light of Advaita — that is, spiritual individualism — playing on and around it; in Europe you are socially individualists, but your thought is dualistic, which is spiritual communism. Thus the one consists of socialist institutions hedged in by individualist thought, while the other is made up of individualist institutions within the hedge of communistic thought.

"Now we must help the Indian experiment as it is. Movements which do not attempt to help things as they are, are, from that point of view, no good. In Europe, for instance, I respect marriage as highly as non-marriage. Never forget that a man is made great and perfect as much by his faults as by his virtues. So we must not seek to rob a nation of its character, even if it could be proved that the character was all faults."

25. "You may always say that the image is God. The error you have to avoid is to think God is the image."

26. The Swami was appealed to on one occasion to condemn the fetishism of the Hottentot. "I do not know", he answered, "what fetishism is!" Then a lurid picture was hastily put before him of the object alternately worshipped, beaten, and thanked. "I do that!" he exclaimed. "Don't you see," he went on, a moment later, in hot

resentment of injustice done to the lowly and absent, "don't you see that there is no fetishism? Oh, your hearts are steeled, that you cannot see that the child is right! The child sees person everywhere. Knowledge robs us of the child's vision. But at last, through higher knowledge, we win back to it. He connects a living power with rocks, sticks, trees and the rest. And is there not a living Power behind them? It is symbolism, not fetishism! Can you not see?"

27. One day he told the story of Satyabhâmâ's sacrifice and how the word "Krishna", written on a piece of paper and thrown into the balance, made Krishna himself, on the other side, kick the beam. "Orthodox Hinduism", he began, "makes Shruti, the sound, everything. The thing is but a feeble manifestation of the pre-existing and eternal idea. So the name of God is everything: God Himself is merely the objectification of that idea in the eternal mind. Your own name is infinitely more perfect than the person you! The name of God is greater than God. Guard your speech!"

28. "I would not worship even the Greek Gods, for they were separate from humanity! Only those should be worshipped who are like ourselves but greater. The difference between the gods and me must be a difference only of degree."

29. "A stone falls and crushes a worm. Hence we infer that all stones, falling, crush worms. Why do we thus immediately reapply a perception? Experience, says one. But it happens, let us suppose, for the first time. Throw a baby into the air, and it cries. Experience from past lives? But why applied to the future? Because there is a real connection between certain things, a pervasiveness, only it lies with us to see that the quality neither overlaps, nor falls short of, the instance. On this discrimination depends all human knowledge.

"With regard to fallacies, it must be remembered that direct perception itself can only be a proof, provided the instrument, the method, and the persistence of the perception are all maintained pure. Disease or emotion will have the effect of disturbing the observation. Therefore direct perception itself is but a mode of inference. Therefore all human knowledge is uncertain and may be erroneous. Who is a true witness? He is a true witness to whom the thing said is a direct perception. Therefore the Vedas are true, because they consist of the evidence of competent persons. But is this power of perception peculiar to any? No! The Rishi, the Aryan, and the Mlechchha all alike have it.

"Modern Bengal holds that evidence is only a special case of direct perception, and that analogy and parity of reasoning are only bad inferences. Therefore, of actual proofs there are only two, direct perception and inference.

"One set of persons, you see, gives priority to the external manifestation, the other to the internal idea. Which is prior, the bird to the egg, or the egg to the bird? Does the oil hold the cup or the cup the oil? This is a problem of which there is no solution. Give it up! Escape from Maya!"

30. "Why should I care if the world itself were to disappear? According to my philosophy, that, you know, would be a very good thing! But, in fact, all that is against me must be with me in the end. Am I not Her soldier?"

31. "Yes, my own life is guided by the enthusiasm of a certain great personality, but what of that? Inspiration was never filtered out to the world through one man!

"It is true I believe Ramakrishna Paramahamsa to have been inspired. But then I am myself inspired also. And you are inspired. And your disciples will be; and theirs after them; and so on, to the end of time!

"Don't you see that the age for esoteric interpretation is over? For good or for ill, that day is vanished, never to return. Truth, in the future, is to be open to the world!"

32. "Buddha made the fatal mistake of thinking that the whole world could be lifted to the height of the Upanishads. And self-interest spoilt all. Krishna was wiser, because He was more politic. But Buddha would have no compromise. The world before now has seen even the Avatâra ruined by compromise, tortured to death for want of recognition, and lost. But Buddha would have been worshipped as God in his own lifetime, all over Asia, for a

moment's compromise. And his reply was only: 'Buddhahood is an achievement, not a person!' Verily was He the only man is the world who was ever quite sane, the only sane man ever born!"

33. People had told the Swami in the West that the greatness of Buddha would have been more appealing, had he been crucified! This he stigmatised as "Roman brutality", and pointed out, "The lowest and most animal liking is for action. Therefore the world will always love the epic. Fortunately for India, however, she has never produced a Milton, with his 'hurled headlong down the steep abyss'! The whole of that were well exchanged for a couple of lines of Browning!" It had been this epic vigour of the story, in his opinion, that had appealed to the Roman. The crucifixion it was that carried Christianity over the Roman world. "Yes, Yes!" he reiterated. "You Western folk want action! You cannot yet perceive the poetry of every common little incident in life! What beauty could be greater than that of the story of the young mother coming to Buddha with her dead boy? Or the incident of the goats? You see the Great Renunciation was not new in India! . . . But after Nirvâna, look at the poetry!

"It is a wet night, and he comes to the cowherd's hut and gathers in to the wall under the dripping eaves. The rain is pouring down and the wind rising. "Within, the cowherd catches a glimpse of a face through the window and thinks, 'Ha, ha! Yellow garb! stay there! It's good enough for you!' And then he begins to sing.

"'My cattle are housed, and the fire burns bright. My wife is safe, and my babes sleep sweet! Therefore ye may rain, if ye will, O clouds, tonight!'

"And the Buddha answers from without, "My mind is controlled: my senses are all gathered in; my heart firm. Therefore ye may rain, if ye will, O clouds, tonight!'

"Again the cowherd: 'The fields are reaped, and the hay is fast in the barn. The stream is full, and the roads are firm. Therefore ye may rain, if ye will, O clouds, tonight.'

"And so it goes on, till at last the cowherd rises, in contrition and wonder, and becomes a disciple.

"Or what would be more beautiful than the barber's story?

The Blessed One passed by my house,

my house — the Barber's!

I ran, but He turned and awaited me, Awaited me — the Barber!

"I said, 'May I speak, O Lord, with Thee?' And He said 'Yes!'

'Yes!' to me — the Barber!

"And I said, 'Is Nirvana for such as I?' And He said 'Yes!'

Even for me — the Barber!

"And I said, 'May I follow after Thee?' And He said, 'Oh yes!'

Even I — the Barber!

And I said, 'May I stay, O Lord, near Thee?' "And He said, 'Thou mayest!'

Even to me — the poor Barber!"

34. "The great point of contrast between Buddhism and Hinduism lies in the fact that Buddhism said, 'Realise all this as illusion', while Hinduism said, 'Realise that within the illusion is the Real.' Of how this was to be done, Hinduism never presumed to enunciate any rigid law. The Buddhist command could only be carried out through monasticism; the Hindu might be fulfilled through any state of life. All alike were roads to the One Real. One of the highest and greatest expressions of the Faith is put into the mouth of a butcher, preaching by the orders of a married woman to a Sannyasin. Thus Buddhism became the religion of a monastic order, but Hinduism, in spite of its exaltation of monasticism, remains ever the religion of faithfulness to duty, whatever it be, as the path by which man may attain God."

35. "Lay down the rules for your group and formulate your ideas," the Swami said, dealing with the monastic ideal for women, "and put in a little universalism, if there is room for it. But remember that not more than half a dozen people in the whole world are ever

at any time ready for this! There must be room for sects, as well as for rising above sects. You will have to manufacture your own tools. Frame laws, but frame them in such a fashion that when people are ready to do without them, they can burst them asunder. Our originality lies in combining perfect freedom with perfect authority. This can be done even in monasticism."

36. "Two different races mix and fuse, and out of them rises one strong distinct type. This tries to save itself from admixture, and here you see the beginning of caste. Look at the apple. The best specimens have been produced by crossing; but once crossed, we try to preserve the variety intact."

37. Referring to education of girls in India he said, "In worship of the gods, you must of course use images. But you can change these. Kali need not always be in one position. Encourage your girls to think of new ways of picturing Her. Have a hundred different conceptions of Saraswati. Let them draw and model and paint their own ideas.

"In the chapel, the pitcher on the lowest step of the altar must be always full of water, and lights in great Tamil butter-lamps must be always burning. If, in addition, the maintenance of perpetual adoration could be organised, nothing could be more in accord with Hindu feeling.

"But the ceremonies employed must themselves be Vedic. There must be a Vedic altar, on which at the hour of worship to light the Vedic fire. And the children must be present to share in the service of oblation. This is a rite which would claim the respect of the whole of India.

"Gather all sorts of animals about you. The cow makes a fine beginning. But you will also have dogs and cats and birds and others. Let the children have a time for going to feed and look after these.

"Then there is the sacrifice of learning. That is the most beautiful of all. Do you know that every book is holy in India, not the Vedas alone, but the English and Mohammedan also? All are sacred.

"Revive the old arts. Teach your girls fruit-modelling with

hardened milk. Give them artistic cooking and sewing. Let them learn painting, photography, the cutting of designs in paper, and gold and silver filigree and embroidery. See that everyone knows something by which she can earn a living in case of need.

"And never forget Humanity! The idea of a humanitarian man-worship exists in nucleus in India, but it has never been sufficiently specialised. Let your students develop it. Make poetry, make art, of it. Yes, a daily worship at the feet of beggars, after bathing and before the meal, would be a wonderful practical training of heart and hand together. On some days, again, the worship might be of children, of your own pupils. Or you might borrow babies and nurse and feed them. What was it that Mâtâji (Tapaswini Mataji, foundress of the Mahâkâli Pâthasâlâ, Calcutta.) said to me? 'Swamiji! I have no help. But these blessed ones I worship, and they will take me to salvation!' She feels, you see, that she is serving Umâ in the Kumâri, and that is a wonderful thought, with which to begin a school."

38. "Love is always a manifestation of bliss. The least shadow of pain falling upon it is always a sign of physicality and selfishness."

39. "The West regards marriage as consisting in all that lies beyond the legal tie, while in India it is thought of as a bond thrown by society round two people to unite them together for all eternity. Those two must wed each other, whether they will or not, in life after life. Each acquires half of the merit of the other. And if one seems in this life to have fallen hopelessly behind, it is for the other only to wait and beat time, till he or she catches up again!"

40. "Consciousness is a mere film between two oceans, the subconscious and the superconscious."

41. "I could not believe my own ears when I heard Western people talking so much of consciousness! Consciousness? What does consciousness matter! Why, it is nothing compared with the unfathomable depths of the subconscious and the heights of the superconscious! In this I could never be misled, for had I not seen Ramakrishna Paramahamsa gather in ten minutes, from a man's subconscious mind, the whole of his past, and determine from that

his future and his powers?"

42. "All these (visions etc.) are side issues. They are not true Yoga. They may have a certain usefulness in establishing indirectly the truth of our statements. Even a little glimpse gives faith that there is something behind gross matter. Yet those who spend time on such things run into grave dangers.

"These (psychic developments) are frontier questions! There can never be any certainty or stability of knowledge reached by their means. Did I not say they were 'frontier questions'? The boundary line is always shifting!"

43. "Now on the Advaitic side it is held that the soul neither comes nor goes, and that all these spheres or layers of the universe are only so many varying products of Âkâsha and Prâna. That is to say, the lowest or most condensed is the Solar Sphere, consisting of the visible universe, in which Prana appears as physical force, and Akasha as sensible matter. The next is called the Lunar Sphere, which surrounds the Solar Sphere. This is not the moon at all, but the habitation of the gods; that is to say, Prana appears in it as psychic forces, and Akasha as Tanmatras or fine particles. Beyond this is the Electric Sphere; that is to say, a condition inseparable from Akasha, and you can hardly tell whether electricity is force or matter. Next is the Brahmaloka, where there is neither Prana nor Akasha, but both are merged into the mind-stuff, the primal energy. And here — there being neither Prana nor Akasha — the Jiva contemplates the whole universe as Samashti or the sum total of Mahat or mind. This appears as Purusha, an abstract Universal Soul, yet not the Absolute, for still there is multiplicity. From this the Jiva finds at last that Unity which is the end. Advaitism says that these are the visions which arise in succession before the Jiva, who himself neither goes nor comes, and that in the same way this present vision has been projected. The projection (Srishti) and dissolution must take place in the same order, only one means going backward and the other coming out.

"Now, as each individual can only see his own universe, that universe is created with his bondage and goes away with his liberation, although it remains for others who are in bondage. Now, name and form constitute the universe. A wave in the ocean is a wave only in so far as it is bound by name and form. If the wave subsides, it is the ocean, but that name-and-form has immediately vanished forever, so that the name and form of a wave could never be without the water that was fashioned into the wave by them. Yet the name and form themselves were not the wave; they die as soon as ever it returns to water, but other names and forms live on in relation to other waves. This name-and-form is called Maya and the water is Brahman. The wave was nothing but water all the time, yet as a wave it had the name and form. Again this name-and-form cannot remain for one moment separated from the wave, although the wave, as water, can remain eternally separate from name and form. But because the name and form can never be separated, they can never be said to exist. Yet they are not zero. This is called Maya."

44. "I am the servant of the servants of the servants of Buddha. Who was there ever like him? — the Lord — who never performed one action for himself — with a heart that embraced the whole world! So full of pity that he — prince and monk — would give his life to save a little goat! So loving that he sacrificed himself to the hunger of a tigress! — to the hospitality of a pariah and blessed him! And he came into my room when I was a boy, and I fell at his feet! For I knew it was the Lord Himself!"

45. "He (Shuka) is the ideal Paramahamsa. To him alone amongst men was it given to drink a handful of the waters of that one undivided Ocean of Sat-Chit- Ânanda — Existence, Knowledge, and Bliss Absolute! Most saints die, having heard only the thunder of its waves upon the shore. A few gain the vision, and still fewer, taste of It. But he drank of the Sea of Bliss!"

46. "What is this idea of Bhakti without renunciation? It is most pernicious."

47. "We worship neither pain nor pleasure. We seek through either to come at that which transcends them both."

48. "Shankaracharya had caught the rhythm of the Vedas, the

national cadence. Indeed I always imagine that he had some vision such as mine when he was young, and recovered the ancient music that way. Anyway, his whole life's work is nothing but that, the throbbing of the beauty of the Vedas and the Upanishads."

49. "Though the love of a mother is in some ways greater, yet the whole world takes the love of man and woman as the type (of the soul's relation to God). No other has such tremendous idealising power. The beloved actually becomes what he is imagined to be. This love transforms its object."

50. "Is it so easy to be Janaka — to sit on a throne absolutely unattached, caring nothing for wealth or fame, for wife or child? One after another in the West has told me that he has reached this. But I could only say, 'Such great men are not born in India!'".

51. "Never forget to say to yourself and to teach to your children, as the difference between a firefly and the blazing sun, between the infinite ocean and a little pond, between a mustard seed and the mountain Meru, such is the difference between the householder and the Sannyasin!

"Everything is fraught with fear: Renunciation alone is fearless.

"Blessed be even the fraudulent Sâdhus and those who have failed to carry out their vows, inasmuch as they also have witnessed to their ideal and so are in some degree the cause of the success of others!

"Let us never, never, forget our ideal!"

52. "The river is pure that flows, the monk is pure that goes!"

53. "The Sannyasin who thinks of gold, to desire it, commits suicide."

54. "What do I care if Mohammed was a good man, or Buddha? Does that altar my goodness or evil? Let us be good for our own sake on our own responsibility."

55. "You people in this country are so afraid of losing your in-di-vid-u-al-i-ty! Why, you are not individuals yet. When you realise

your whole nature, you will attain your true individuality, not before. There is another thing I am constantly hearing in this country, and that is that we should live in harmony with nature. Don't you know that all the progress ever made in the world was made by conquering nature? We are to resist nature at every point if we are to make any progress."

56. "In India they tell me I ought not to teach Advaita Vedanta to the people at large; but I say, I can make even a child understand it. You cannot begin too early to teach the highest spiritual truths."

57. "The less you read, the better. Read the Gita and other good works on Vedanta. That is all you need. The present system of education is all wrong. The mind is crammed with facts before it knows how to think. Control of the mind should be taught first. If I had my education to get over again and had any voice in the matter, I would learn to master my mind first, and then gather facts if I wanted them. It takes people a long time to learn things because they can't concentrate their minds at will."

58. "If a bad time comes, what of that? The pendulum must swing back to the other side. But that is no better. The thing to do is to stop it."

Part- III

SAYINGS AND UTTERANCES

List Of Abbreviations

In this section, only Swami Vivekananda's direct words have been placed within quotation marks. References have been identified by the following abbreviations:

ND Burke, Marie Louise. Swami Vivekananda in the West: New Discoveries. 6 vols. Calcutta: Advaita Ashrama, 1983-87.

CWSN Nivedita, Sister. The Complete Works of Sister Nivedita. Vol. 1. Calcutta: Advaita Ashrama, 1982.

LSN Nivedita, Sister. Letters of Sister Nivedita. 2 vols. Compiled and edited by Sankari Prasad Basu. Calcutta: Nababharat Publishers, 1982.

VIN Basu, Sankari Prasad and Ghosh, Sunil Bihari, eds. Vivekananda in Indian Newspapers: 1893-1902. Calcutta: Dineshchandra Basu, Basu Bhattacharya and Co., 1969.

1. From Mrs. Prince Woods's description of Swami Vivekananda's departure from the Woods's residence in Salem, Massachusetts, in August 1893. Swami Vivekananda gave his staff, his most precious possession, to Dr. Woods, who was at that time a young medical student, and his trunk and his blanket to Mrs. Kate T.

Woods, saying:

"Only my most precious possessions should I give to my friends who have made me at home in this great country." (ND 1: 42)

2. On the back of Swami Vivekananda's transcription from Louis Rousselet's book India and Its Native Princes — Travels in Central India and in the Presidencies of Bombay and Bengal, dated February 11, 1894:

"I say there is but one remedy for one too anxious for the future — to go down on his knees." (ND 1: 225)

3. An extract from a prayer Swami Vivekananda delivered at the Chicago World's Parliament of Religions:

"Thou art He that beareth the burdens of the universe; help me to bear the little burden of this life." (ND 2: 32)

4. An extract from another prayer offered by Swami Vivekananda at the Chicago World's Parliament of Religions:

"At the head of all these laws, in and through every particle of matter and force, stands One through whose command the wind blows, the fire burns, the clouds rain, and death stalks upon the earth. And what is His nature? He is everywhere the pure and formless One, the Almighty and the All Merciful. Thou art our Father. Thou art our beloved Friend." (ND 2: 33)

5. From Mary T. Wright's journal entry dated Saturday, May 12, 1894:

The widows of high caste in India do not marry, he said; only the widows of low caste may marry, may eat, drink, dance, have as many husbands as they choose, divorce them all, in short enjoy all the benefits of the highest society in this country. . . .

"When we are fanatical", he said, "we torture ourselves, we throw ourselves under huge cars, we cut our throats, we lie on spiked beds; but when you are fanatical you cut other people's throats, you torture them by fire and put them on spiked beds! You take very good care of your own skins!" (ND 2: 58-59)

6. An 1894 extract from the Greenacre Voice, quoting one of the Swami's teachings delivered at Greenacre, Maine:

"You and I and everything in the universe are that Absolute, not parts, but the whole. You are the whole of that Absolute." (ND 2: 150)

7. In a March 5, 1899 letter from Sister Nivedita to Miss Josephine MacLeod:

"I am at heart a mystic, Margot, all this reasoning is only apparent — I am really always on the lookout for signs and things — and so I never bother about the fate of my initiations. If they want to be Sannyâsins badly enough I feel that the rest is not my business. Of course it has its bad side. I have to pay dearly for my blunder sometimes — but it has one advantage. It has kept me still a Sannyasin through all this — and that is my ambition, to die a real Sannyasin as Ramakrishna Paramahamsa actually was — free from lust — and desire of wealth, and thirst for fame. That thirst for fame is the worst of all filth." (ND 3: 128-29)

8. From John Henry Wright's March 27, 1896 letter to Mary Tappan Wright, in which Swami Vivekananda stated that England is just like India with its castes:

"I had to have separate classes for the two castes. For the high caste people — Lady This and Lady That, Honourable This and Honourable That — I had classes in the morning; for the low caste people, who came pell-mell, I had classes in the evening." (ND 4: 73)

9. While Swami Vivekananda was offering flowers at the feet of the Virgin Mary in a small chapel in Switzerland in the summer of 1896, he said:

"For she also is the Mother." (ND 4: 276)

10. From Mr. J. J. Goodwin's October 23, 1896 letter to Mrs. Ole Bull, quoting Swami Vivekananda's conversation at Greycoat Gardens in London

"It is very good to have a high ideal, but don't make it too high. A high ideal raises mankind, but an impossible ideal lowers them from the very impossibility of the case." (ND 4: 385)

11. A November 20, 1896 entry from Swami Abhedananda's diary, quoting Swami Vivekananda's observation of the English people:

"You can't make friends here without knowing their customs, behaviour, politics. You have to know the manners of the rich, the cultured and the poor." (ND 4: 478)

12. In Mr. J. J. Goodwin's November 11, 1896 letter to Mrs. Ole Bull, quoting Swami Vivekananda's unpublished statement toward the end of "Practical Vedanta — IV":

"A Jiva can never attain absolutely to Brahman until the whole of Mâyâ disappears. While there is still a Jiva left in Maya, there can be no soul absolutely free Vedantists are divided on this point." (ND 4: 481)

13. From Swami Saradananda's letter to a brother-disciple, concerning Swami Vivekananda's last days:

Sometimes he would say, "Death has come to my bedside; I have been through enough of work and play; let the world realize what contribution I have made; it will take quite a long time to understand that". (ND 4: 521)

14. In an October 13, 1898 letter to Mrs. Ashton Jonson, written from Kashmir, Sister Nivedita described Swami Vivekananda's spiritual mood:

To him at this moment "doing good" seems horrible. "Only the Mother does anything. Patriotism is a mistake. Everything is a mistake. It is all Mother. . . .

All men are good. Only we cannot reach all. . . . I am never going to teach any more. Who am I that I should teach anyone? . . . Swamiji is dead and gone." (ND 5: 3-4)

15. From Mr. Sachindranath Basu's letter recounting Swami Vivekananda's closing remarks in his talk to swamis and novices assembled at Belur Math, June 19, 1899:

"My sons, all of you be men. This is what I want! If you are even a little successful, I shall feel my life has been meaningful." (ND 5: 17)

16. During an evening talk with Swami Saradananda in the spring of 1899: "Men should be taught to be practical, physically strong. A dozen such lions will conquer the world, not millions of sheep. Men should not be taught to imitate a personal ideal, however great." (ND 5: 17)

17. From Mrs. Mary C. Funke's reminiscences of her August 1899 voyage to America with Swamis Vivekananda and Turiyananda:

"And if all this Maya is so beautiful, think of the wondrous beauty of the Reality behind it!" (ND 5: 76)

"Why recite poetry when there [pointing to sea and sky] is the very essence of poetry?" (Ibid.)

18. In Miss Josephine MacLeod's September 3, 1899 letter to Mrs. Ole Bull:

"In one's greatest hour of need one stands alone." (ND 5: 122)

19. From Sister Nivedita's October 27, 1899 diary entry at Ridgely Manor, in which Swami Vivekananda expressed his concern for Olea Bull Vaughn: "Nightmares always begin pleasantly — only at the worst point [the] dream is broken — so death breaks [the] dream of life. Love death." (ND 5: 138)

20. In a December 1899 letter from Miss Josephine MacLeod to Sister Nivedita:

"All the ideas the Californians have of me emanated from Chicago." (ND 5: 179)

21. From Mrs. Alice Hansbrough's reminiscences which quoted Swami Vivekananda as telling Mr. Baumgardt:

"I can talk on the same subject, but it will not be the same lecture." (ND 5: 230)

22. Mrs. Alice Hansbrough's reminiscences relating Swami

Vivekananda's response to her sight-seeing attempts:

"Do not show me sights. I have seen the Himalayas! I would not go ten steps to see sights; but I would go a thousand miles to see a [great] human being!" (ND 5: 244)

23. From Mrs. Alice Hansbrough's reminiscences relating Swami Vivekananda's interest in the problem of child training:

He did not believe in punishment. It had never helped him, he said, and added, "I would never do anything to make a child afraid". (ND 5: 253)

24. Mrs. Alice Hansbrough's record of Swami Vivekananda's explanation of God to seventeen-year-old Ralph Wyckoff:

"Can you see your own eyes? God is like that. He is as close as your own eyes. He is your own, even though you can't see Him." (ND 5: 254)

25. Mrs. Alice Hansbrough's reminiscences regarding Swami Vivekananda's opinion of the low-caste English soldiers who occupied India:

"If anyone should despoil the Englishman's home, the Englishman would kill him, and rightly so. But the Hindu just sits and whines!

"Do you think that a handful of Englishmen could rule India if we had a militant spirit? I teach meat-eating throughout the length and breadth of India in the hope that we can build a militant spirit!" (ND 5: 256)

26. Mrs. Alice Hansbrough's reminiscences of a picnic in Pasadena, California when a Christian Science woman suggested to Swami Vivekananda that one should teach people to be good:

"Why should I desire to be 'good'? All this is His handiwork [waving his hand to indicate the trees and the countryside]. Shall I apologize for His handiwork? If you want to reform John Doe, go and live with him; don't try to reform him. If you have any of the Divine Fire, he will catch it." (ND 5: 257)

27. From Mrs. Alice Hansbrough's reminiscences:

"When once you consider an action, do not let anything dissuade you. Consult your heart, not others, and then follow its dictates." (ND 5: 311)

28. From Mr. Frank Rhodehamel's notes taken during a March 1900 lecture in Oakland, California:

"Never loved a husband the wife for the wife's sake, or the wife the husband for the husband's sake. It is God in the wife the husband loves, and God in the husband the wife loves. (Cf. Brihadâranyaka Upanishad II.4.5.) It is God in everyone that draws us to that one in love. [It is] God in everything, in everybody that makes us love. God is the only love In everyone is God, the

Atman; all else is but dream, an illusion." (ND 5: 362)

29. From Mr. Frank Rhodehamel's notes taken during a March 1900 lecture in Oakland, California:

Oh, if you only knew yourselves! You are souls; you are gods. If ever I feel [that I am] blaspheming, it is when I call you man." (ND 5: 362)

30. An excerpt from Mr. Thomas J. Allan's reminiscences of Swami Vivekananda's March 1900 San Francisco lecture series on India:

"Send us mechanics to teach us how to use our hands, and we will send you missionaries to teach you spirituality." (ND 5: 365)

31. Mrs. Edith Allan's reminiscences of Swami Vivekananda's philosophical observations while cooking at the Turk Street flat:

"'The Lord dwells in the hearts of all beings, O Arjuna, by His illusive power causing all beings to revolve as though mounted on a potter's wheel.' [Bhagavad-Gitâ XVIII.61] This has all happened before, like the throw of a dice, so it is in life; the wheel goes on and the same combination comes up; that pitcher and glass have stood there before, so, too, that onion and potato. What can we do, Madam, He has us on the wheel of life." (ND 6: 17)

32. From Mrs. Edith Allan's reminiscences of an after-lunch conversation:

"The Master said he would come again in about two hundred years — and I will come with him. When a Master comes, he brings his own people." (ND 6: 17)

33. Mrs. Edith Allan's reminiscences of Swami Vivekananda's "kitchen" counsel while he was staying in San Francisco, California, in 1900:

"If I consider myself greater than the ant that crawls on the ground I am ignorant." (ND 6: 19)

"Madam, be broad—minded; always see two ways. When I am on the heights I say, 'Shivoham, Shivoham: I am He, I am He!' and when I have the stomachache I say, 'Mother have mercy on me!'" (Ibid.)

"Learn to be the witness. If two dogs are fighting on the street and I go out there, I get mixed up in the fight; but if I stay quietly in my room, I witness the fight from the window. So learn to be the witness." (Ibid.)

34. From Mr. Thomas J. Allan's reminiscences of a private talk with Swami Vivekananda in San Francisco, California, 1900:

"We do not progress from error to truth, but from truth to truth. Thus we must see that none can be blamed for what they are doing, because they are, at this time, doing the best they can. If a child has an open razor, don't try to take it from him, but give him a red apple or a brilliant toy, and he will drop the razor. But he who puts his hand in the fire will be burned; we learn only from experience." (ND 6: 42)

35. From Mrs. Alice Hansbrough's reminiscences of a walk home with Swami Vivekananda after one of his lectures in San Francisco in 1900:

"You have heard that Christ said, 'My words are spirit and they are life'. So are my words spirit and life; they will burn their way into your brain and you will never get away from them!" (ND 6: 57-58)

36. From Mrs. Alice Hansbrough's reminiscences in San Francisco, 1900 — referring to Swami Vivekananda's great heart:

"I may have to be born again because I have fallen in love with man." (ND 6: 79)

37. From Mrs. George Roorbach's reminiscences of Swami Vivekananda at Camp Taylor, California, in May 1900:

"In my first speech in this country, in Chicago, I addressed that audience as 'Sisters and Brothers of America', and you know that they all rose to their feet. You may wonder what made them do this, you may wonder if I had some strange power. Let me tell you that I did have a power and this is it — never once in my life did I allow myself to have even one sexual thought. I trained my mind, my thinking, and the powers that man usually uses along that line I put into a higher channel, and it developed a force so strong that nothing could resist it." (ND 6: 155)

38. In a conversation with Swami Turiyananda, which probably took place in New York:

"The call has come from Above: 'Come away, just come away — no need of troubling your head to teach others'. It is now the will of the Grand Old Lady (The "Grand Old Lady" was a figure in a children's game, whose touch put one outside the game.) that the play should be over." (ND 6: 373)

39. In a July 1902 Prabuddha Bharata eulogy, "a Western disciple" wrote: The Swami had but scant sympathy with iconoclasts, for as he wisely remarked, "The true philosopher strives to destroy nothing, but to help all". (VIN: 638)

40. Sister Nivedita's reminiscences of Swami Vivekananda in an October 9, 1899 letter to Miss Josephine MacLeod:

He has turned back on so much — "Let your life in the world be nothing but a thinking to yourself". (LSN I: 213)

41. Swami Vivekananda's luncheon remarks to Mrs. Ole Bull, recorded by Sister Nivedita in an October 18, 1899 letter to Miss Josephine MacLeod:

"You see, there is one thing called love, and there is another thing called union. And union is greater than love.

"I do not love religion. I have become identified with it. It is my life. So no man loves that thing in which his life has been spent, in which he really has accomplished something. That which we love is not yet ourself. Your husband did not love music for which he had always stood. He loved engineering in which as yet he knew comparatively little. This is the difference between Bhakti and Jnana; and this is why Jnana is greater than Bhakti." (LSN I: 216)

42. Swami Vivekananda's remarks on his spiritual ministry, recorded in Sister Nivedita's October 15, 1904 letter to Miss Josephine MacLeod:

"Only when they go away will they know how much they have received." (LSN II: 686)

43. Sister Nivedita's reminiscences in a November 5, 1904 letter to Alberta Sturges (Lady Sandwich) of Swami Vivekananda's talk on renunciation while he was staying at Ridgely Manor:

"In India we never say that you should renounce a higher thing for a lower. It is better to be absorbed in music or in literature than in comfort or pleasure, and we never say otherwise." (LSN II: 690)

44. In Sister Nivedita's November 19, 1909 letter to Miss Josephine MacLeod:

"The fire burns if we plunge our hand in — whether we feel it or not — so it is with him who speaks the name of God." (LSN II: 1030)

45. Swami Vivekananda's reminiscences of Shri Ramakrishna, recorded in Sister Nivedita's July 6, 1910 letter to Dr. T. K. Cheyne:

"He could not imagine himself the teacher of anyone. He was like a man playing with balls of many colours, and leaving it to others to select which they would for themselves." (LSN II: 1110)

46. Sister Nivedita's reminiscences of a conversation with Swami Vivekananda at Ridgely Manor, recorded in an 1899 letter

written from Ridgely Manor to Miss Josephine MacLeod:

I have never heard the Prophet talk so much of Shri Ramakrishna. He told us what I had heard before of [his master's] infallible judgement of men. . . .

"And so", Swami said, "you see my devotion is the dog's devotion. I have been wrong so often and he has always been right, and now I trust his judgement blindly". And then he told us how he would hypnotize anyone who came to him and in two minutes know all about him, and Swami said that from this he had learnt to count our consciousness as a very small thing. (LSN II: 1263)

47. From Sister Nivedita's January 27, 1900 letter to Sister Christine: Swami said today that he is beginning to see the needs of humanity in quite a different light — that he is already sure of the principle that is to help, but is spending hours every day in trying to solve the methods. That what he had known hitherto is for men living in a cave — alone, undisturbed — but now he will give "humanity something that will make for strength in the stress of daily life". (LSN II: 1264)

48. In a July 7, 1902 letter to Sister Christine, Sister Nivedita recorded one of Swami Vivekananda's remarks made while giving a class to the monks at Belur Math on July 4, 1902:

"Do not copy me. Kick out the man who imitates." (LSN II: 1270)

49. The Swami's comment after he made a statement concerning the ideal of the freedom of the soul, which brought it into apparent conflict with the Western conception of the service of humanity as the goal of the individual:

"You will say that this does not benefit society. But before this objection can be admitted you will first have to prove that the maintenance of society is an object in itself." (CWSN 1: 19)

50. Sister Nivedita wrote:

He touched on the question of his own position as a wandering teacher and expressed the Indian diffidence with regard to religious organization or, as someone expresses it, "with regard to a faith that ends in a church". "We believe", he said, "that organization always breeds new evils".

He prophesied that certain religious developments then much in vogue in the West would speedily die, owing to love of money. And he declared that "Man proceeds from truth to truth, and not from error to truth". (CWSN 1: 19-20)

51. "The universe is like a cobweb and minds are the spiders; for mind is one as well as many." (CWSN 1: 21)

52. "Let none regret that they were difficult to convince! I fought my Master for six years with the result that I know every inch of the way! Every inch of the way!" (CWSN 1: 22)

53. Swami Vivekananda was elucidating to what heights of selflessness the path of love leads and how it draws out the very best faculties of the soul: "Suppose there were a baby in the path of the tiger! Where would your place be then? At his mouth — any one of you — I am sure of it." (CWSN 1: 24)

54. "That by which all this is pervaded, know That to be the Lord Himself!" (CWSN 1: 27)

55. Concerning Swami Vivekananda's attitude toward religion:

Religion was a matter of the growth of the individual, "a question always of being and becoming". (CWSN 1: 28)

56. "Forgive when you also can bring legions of angels to an easy victory." While victory was still doubtful, however, only a coward to his thinking would turn the other cheek. (CWSN 1: 28-29)

57. "Of course I would commit a crime and go to hell forever if by that I could really help a human being!" (CWSN 1: 34)

58. To a small group, including Sister Nivedita, after a lecture:

"I have a superstition — it is nothing, you know, but a personal superstition! — that the same soul who came once as Buddha came afterwards as Christ." (CWSN 1: 35)

59. After Swami Vivekananda was told of Sister Nivedita's

willingness to serve India:

"For my own part I will be incarnated two hundred times, if that is necessary, to do this work amongst my people that I have undertaken." (CWSN 1: 36)

60. Sister Nivedita's memory of an incident:

He was riding on one occasion with the Raja of Khetri, when he saw that his arm was bleeding profusely and found that the wound had been caused by a thorny branch which he had held aside for himself to pass. When the Swami expostulated, the Rajput laughed the matter aside. "Are we not always the defenders of the faith, Swamiji?" he said.

"And then", said the Swami, telling the story, "I was just going to tell him that they ought not to show such honour to the Sannyasin, when suddenly I thought that perhaps they were right after all. Who knows? Maybe I too am caught in the glare of this flashlight of your modern civilization, which is only for a moment".

" — I have become entangled", he said simply to one who protested that to his mind the wandering Sâdhu of earlier years, who had scattered his knowledge and changed his name as he went, had been greater than the abbot of Belur, burdened with much work and many cares. "I have become entangled." (CWSN 1: 43)

61. Sister Nivedita wrote:

One day he was talking in the West of Mirâ Bâi — that saint who once upon a time was Queen of Chitore — and of the freedom her husband had offered her if only she would remain within the royal seclusion. But she could not be bound. "But why should she not?" someone asked in astonishment. "Why should she?" he retorted. "Was she living down here in this mire?" (CWSN 1: 44)

62. As years went by, the Swami dared less and less to make determinate plans or dogmatize about the unknown:

"After all, what do we know? Mother uses it all. But we are only fumbling about." (CWSN 1: 44)

63. Quoting Swami Vivekananda, Sister Nivedita remembered:

Love was not love, it was insisted, unless it was "without a reason" or without a "motive" (CWSN 1: 52)

64. About Swami Vivekananda, Sister Nivedita wrote:

When asked by some of his own people what he considered, after seeing them in their own country, to be the greatest achievement of the English, he answered "that they had known how to combine obedience with self-respect". (CWSN 1: 54)

65. Swami Sadananda reported that early in the morning, while it was still dark, Swami Vivekananda would rise and call the others, singing:

"Awake! Awake! all ye who would drink of the divine nectar!" (CWSN 1: 56)

66. Sister Nivedita remembered:

At this time [during the Swami's itinerant days, near Almora] he passed some months in a cave overhanging a mountain village. Only twice have I known him to allude to this experience. Once he said, "Nothing in my whole life ever so filled me with the sense of work to be done. It was as if I were thrown out from that life in caves to wander to and fro in the plains below". And again he said to someone, "It is not the form of his life that makes a Sadhu. For it is possible to sit in a cave and have one's whole mind filled with the question of how many pieces of bread will be brought to one for supper!" (CWSN 1: 61)

67. About his own poem "Kali the Mother":

"Scattering plagues and sorrows", he quoted from his own verses, Dancing mad with joy,

Come, Mother, come! For terror is Thy name! Death — is in Thy breath. And every shaking step

Destroys a world for e'er.

"It all came true, every word of it", he interrupted himself to say.

Who dares misery love. Dance in Destruction's dance, And hug the form of death, . . .

"To him the Mother does indeed come. I have proved it. For I have hugged the form of Death!" (CWSN 1: 98-99)

68. Sister Nivedita, referring to her plans for a girls' school:

Only in one respect was he [Swami Vivekananda] inflexible. The work for the education of Indian women, to which he would give his name, might be as sectarian as I chose to make it. "You wish through a sect to rise beyond all sects." (CWSN 1: 102)

69. Commenting on Sister Nivedita's visit to Gopaler-Ma's dwelling — a small cell:

"Ah! this is the old India that you have seen, the India of prayers and tears, of vigils and fasts, that is passing away, never to return!" (CWSN 1: 109)

70. About the aims of the Ramakrishna Order:

The same purpose spoke again in his definition of the aims of the Order of Ramakrishna — "to effect an exchange of the highest ideals of the East and the West and to realize these in practice" (CWSN 1: 113)

71. After teaching Sister Nivedita the worship of Shiva, Swami Vivekananda then culminated it in an offering of flowers at the feet of the Buddha. He said, as if addressing each soul that would ever come to him for guidance:

"Go thou and follow Him, who was born and gave His life for others five hundred times before He attained the vision of the Buddha!" (CWSN 1: 114)

72. Upon returning from a pilgrimage in Kashmir:

"These gods are not merely symbols! They are the forms that the Bhaktas have seen!" (CWSN 1: 120)

73. Sister Nivedita's reminiscences of Swami Vivekananda's words heard long before:

"The Impersonal God seen through the mists of sense is

personal." (CWSN 1: 120)

74. Swami Vivekananda's comment when he was reminded of the rareness of criminality in India:

"Would God it were otherwise in my land, for this is verily the virtuousness of death!" (CWSN 1: 123)

75. Swami Vivekananda said:

"The whole of life is only a swan song! Never forget those lines: The lion, when stricken to the heart, gives out his mightiest roar.

When smitten on the head, the cobra lifts its hood. And the majesty of the soul comes forth, only when a man is wounded to his depths."

(CWSN 1: 124)

76. After hearing of the death of Shri Durga Charan Nag (Nag Mahashay): "[He] was one of the greatest of the works of Ramakrishna Paramahamsa." (CWSN 1: 129)

77. About Shri Ramakrishna's transformative power, Swami Vivekananda said:

"Was it a joke that Ramakrishna Paramahamsa should touch a life? Of course he made new men and new women of those who came to him, even in these fleeting contacts!" (CWSN 1: 130)

78. While speaking on the true spirit of a Sannyasin, Swami Vivekananda said:

"I saw many great men in Hrishikesh. One case that I remember was that of a man who seemed to be mad. He was coming nude down the street, with boys pursuing and throwing stones at him. The whole man was bubbling over with laughter while blood was streaming down his face and neck. I took him and bathed the wound, putting ashes on it to stop the bleeding. And all the time with peals of laughter he told me of the fun the boys and he had been having, throwing the stones. 'So the Father plays', he said.

"Many of these men hide, in order to guard themselves against intrusion. People are a trouble to them. One had human bones strewn about his cave and gave it out that he lived on corpses. Another threw stones. And so on. . . .

"Sometimes the thing comes upon them in a flash. There was a boy, for instance, who used to come to read the Upanishads with Abhedananda. One day he turned and said, 'Sir, is all this really true?'

"'Oh yes!' said Abhedananda, 'It may be difficult to realize, but it is certainly true'.

"And next day, that boy was a silent Sannyasin, nude, on his way to Kedarnath! "What happened to him? you ask. He became silent!

"But the Sannyasin needs no longer to worship or to go on pilgrimage or perform austerities. What then is the motive of all this going from pilgrimage to pilgrimage, shrine to shrine, and austerity to austerity? He is acquiring merit and giving it to the world!" (CWSN 1: 133)

79. Referring to the story of Shibi Rana:

"Ah yes! These are the stories that are deep in our nation's heart! Never forget that the Sannyasin takes two vows: one to realize the truth and one to help the world — and that the most stringent of stringent requirements is that he should renounce any thought of heaven!" (CWSN 1: 134)

80. To Sister Nivedita:

"The Gitâ says that there are three kinds of charity: the Tâmasic, the Râjasic and the Sâttvic. Tamasic charity is performed on an impulse. It is always making mistakes. The doer thinks of nothing but his own impulse to be kind. Rajasic charity is what a man does for his own glory. And Sattvic charity is that which is given to the right person, in the right way, and at the proper time. . . .

"When it comes to the Sattvic, I think more and more of a certain great Western woman in whom I have seen that quiet giving, always to the right person in the right way, at the right time, and never making a mistake.

"For my own part, I have been learning that even charity can go too far. . . .

"As I grow older I find that I look more and more for greatness in little things. I want to know what a great man eats and wears, and how he speaks to his servants. I want to find a Sir Philip Sidney (Sir Philip Sidney (1554 -1586): English poet, soldier and politician.) greatness! Few men would remember the thirst of others, even in the moment of death.

"But anyone will be great in a great position! Even the coward will grow brave in the glare of the footlights. The world looks on. Whose heart will not throb?

Whose pulse will not quicken till he can do his best?

"More and more the true greatness seems to me that of the worm doing its duty silently, steadily, from moment to moment and from hour to hour." (CWSN 1: 137)

81. Referring to the great individual — the divine incarnation, the Guru, and the Rishi:

"You do not yet understand India! We Indians are man — worshippers, after all! Our God is man!" (CWSN 1: 144)

82. On another occasion, Swami Vivekananda used the word "man- worshippers" in an entirely different sense:

"This idea of man—worship exists in nucleus in India, but it has never been expanded. You must develop it. Make poetry, make art, of it. Establish the worship of the feet of beggars as you had it in Mediaeval Europe. Make man- worshippers." (CWSN 1: 144-45)

83. To Sister Nivedita:

"There is a peculiar sect of Mohammedans who are reported to be so fanatical that they take each newborn babe and expose it, saying, 'If God made thee, perish! If Ali made thee, live!' Now this, which they say to the child, I say, but in the opposite sense, to you tonight: 'Go forth into the world and there, if I made you, be destroyed! If Mother made you, live'!" (CWSN 1: 151)

84. Long after Southern magnates in America had apologized

to Vivekananda when they learned that he had been mistaken for a Negro and was thus refused admission into hotels, the Swami remarked to himself:

"What! rise at the expense of another! I didn't come to earth for that! . . . If I am grateful to my white-skinned Aryan ancestor, I am far more so to my yellow- skinned Mongolian ancestor and, most so of all, to the black-skinned Negritoid!" (CWSN 1: 153)

85. Commenting on the dungeon-cages of mediaeval prisoners on Mont- Saint-Michel:

"What a wonderful place for meditation!" (CWSN 1: 154)

"Oh, I know I have wandered over the whole earth, but in India I have looked for nothing save the cave in which to meditate!" (Ibid.)

86. Though he considered offspring of the Roman Empire to be brutal and the Japanese notion of marriage a horror, Swami Vivekananda nevertheless summed up the constructive ideals, never the defects, of a community:

"For patriotism, the Japanese! For purity, the Hindu! And for manliness, the European! There is no other in the world who understands, as does the Englishman, what should be the glory of a man!" (CWSN 1: 160)

87. Swami Vivekananda said of himself before he left for America in 1893: "I go forth to preach a religion of which Buddhism is nothing but a rebel child and Christianity, with all her pretensions, only a distant echo!" (CWSN 1: 161)

88. Describing the night Buddha left his wife to renounce the world, Swami Vivekananda said:

"What was the problem that vexed him? Why! It was she whom he was about to sacrifice for the world! That was the struggle! He cared nothing for himself!" (CWSN 1: 172)

89. After describing Buddha's touching farewell to his wife, the Swami said: "Have you never thought of the hearts of the heroes? How they were great, great, great — and soft as butter?" (CWSN 1: 172)

90. Swami Vivekananda's description of Buddha's death and its similarity with that of Shri Ramakrishna's:

He told how the blanket had been spread for him beneath the tree and how the Blessed One had lain down, "resting on his right side like a lion" to die, when suddenly there came to him one who ran for instruction. The disciples would have treated the man as an intruder, maintaining peace at any cost about their Master's death-bed, but the Blessed One overheard, and saying, "No, no! He who was sent (Lit., "the Tathâgata". "A word", explained Swami Vivekananda, "which is very like your 'Messiah'".) is ever ready", he raised himself on his elbow and taught. This happened four times and then, and then only, Buddha held himself free to die. "But first he spoke to reprove Ananda for weeping. The Buddha was not a person but a realization, and to that any one of them might attain. And with his last breath he forbade them to worship any."

The immortal story went on to its end. But to one who listened, the most significant moment had been that in which the teller paused — at his own words "raised himself on his elbow and taught" — and said, in brief parenthesis, "I saw this, you know, in the case of Ramakrishna Paramahamsa". And there rose before the mind the story of one, destined to learn from that teacher, who had travelled a hundred miles, and arrived at Cossipore only when he lay dying. Here also the disciples would have refused admission, but Shri Ramakrishna intervened, insisting on receiving the new-comer, and teaching him. (CWSN 1: 175-176)

91. Commenting on the historic and philosophic significance of Buddhistic doctrine:

"Form, feeling, sensation, motion and knowledge are the five categories in perpetual flux and fusion. And in these lies Maya. Of any one wave nothing can be predicated, for it is not. It but was and is gone. Know, O Man, thou art the sea! Ah, this was Kapila's philosophy, but his great disciple [Buddha] brought the heart to make it live!" (CWSN 1: 176)

92. Concerning the Buddhist First Council and the dispute as to its President:

"Can you imagine what their strength was? One said it should be Ananda, because he had loved Him most. But someone else stepped forward and said no! for Ananda had been guilty of weeping at the death-bed. And so he was passed over!" (CWSN 1: 177)

93. Considering reincarnation a "scientific speculation" rather than an article of faith:

"Why, one life in the body is like a million years of confinement, and they want to wake up the memory of many lives! Sufficient unto the day is the evil thereof! . . . Yes! Buddhism must be right! Reincarnation is only a mirage! But this vision is to be reached by the path of Advaita alone!" (CWSN 1: 180-81)

94. "Had I lived in Palestine, in the days of Jesus of Nazareth, I would have washed his feet, not with my tears, but with my heart's blood!" (CWSN 1: 189)

95. "For the Advaitin, therefore, the only motive is love. . . . It is the Saviour who should go on his way rejoicing, not the saved!" (CWSN 1: 197- 98)

96. On the necessity of restraint in a disciple's life:

"Struggle to realize yourself without a trace of emotion! . . . Watch the fall of the leaves, but gather the sentiment of the sight from within at some later time!" (CWSN 1: 207)

"Mind! No loaves and fishes! No glamour of the world! All this must be cut short. It must be rooted out. It is sentimentality—the overflow of the senses. It comes to you in colour, sight, sound, and associations. Cut it off. Learn to hate it. It is utter poison!" (Ibid., 207-208)

97. On the value of types:

"Two diffferent races mix and fuse, and out of them rises one strong distinct type. A strong and distinct type is always the physical basis of the horizon. It is all very well to talk of universalism, but the world will not be ready for that for millions of years!

"Remember! if you want to know what a ship is like, the ship has to be specified as it is — its length, breadth, shape, and material. And to understand a nation, we must do the same. India is idolatrous. You must help her as she is.

Those who have left her can do nothing for her!" (CWSN 1: 209)

98. Describing the Indian ideal of Brahmacharya in the student's life, Swami Vivekananda said:

"Brahmacharya should be like a burning fire within the veins!" (CWSN 1: 216)

99. Concerning marriage by arrangement instead of choice, Swami Vivekananda said:

"There is such pain in this country! Such pain! Some, of course, there must always have been. But now the sight of Europeans with their different customs has increased it. Society knows that there is another way!

[To a European] "We have exalted motherhood and you, wifehood; and I think both might gain by some interchange.

"In India the wife must not dream of loving even a son as she loves her husband. She must be Sati. But the husband ought not to love his wife as he does his mother. Hence a reciprocated affection is not thought so high as one unreturned. It is 'shopkeeping'. The joy of the contact of husband and wife is not admitted in India. This we have to borrow from the West. Our ideal needs to be refreshed by yours. And you, in turn, need something of our devotion to motherhood." (CWSN 1: 221-22)

100.Speaking to a disciple with great compassion:

"You need not mind if these shadows of home and marriage cross your mind sometimes. Even to me, they come now and again!" (CWSN 1: 222)

101.On hearing of the intense loneliness of a friend:

"Every worker feels like that at times!" (CWSN 1: 222)

102.Concerning the Hindu and Buddhist monastic and non-monastic ideals: "The glory of Hinduism lies in the fact that while it has defined ideals, it has never dared to say that any one of these alone was the one true way. In this it differs from Buddhism, which exalts monasticism above all others as the path that must be taken by all souls to reach perfection. The story given in the Mahâbhârata of the young saint who was made to seek enlightenment, first from a married woman and then from a butcher, is sufficient to show this. 'By doing my duty', said each one of these when asked, 'by doing my duty in my own station, have I attained this knowledge'. There is no career then which might not be the path to God. The question of attainment depends only, in the last resort, on the thirst of the soul." (CWSN 1: 223)

103.With reference to the idea that the lover always sees the ideal in the beloved, Swami Vivekananda responded to a girl's newly avowed love:

"Cling to this vision! As long as you can both see the ideal in one another, your worship and happiness will grow more instead of less." (CWSN 1: 224)

104."The highest truth is always the simplest." (CWSN 1: 226)

105.Swami Vivekananda's remarks on American séances:

"Always the greatest fraud by the simplest means." (CWSN 1: 233)

106.On Western and Eastern views of a person as a body or a soul:

"Western languages declare that man is a body and has a soul; Eastern languages declare that he is a soul and has a body." (CWSN 1: 236-37)

107.Concerning Swami Vivekananda's reverence for his Guru:

"I can criticize even an Avatâra [divine incarnation] without the slightest diminution of my love for him! But I know quite well that most people are not so; and for them it is safest to protect their own Bhakti!" (CWSN 1: 252)

"Mine is the devotion of the dog! I don't want to know why! I am contented simply to follow!" (Ibid., 252-53)

108."Ramakrishna Paramahamsa used to begin every day by walking about in his room for a couple of hours, saying 'Satchidânanda!' or 'Shivoham!' or some other holy word." (CWSN 1: 255)

109.A few months before his passing away, Swami Vivekananda said:

"How often does a man ruin his disciples by remaining always with them! When men are once trained, it is essential that their leader leaves them; for without his absence they cannot develop themselves!" (CWSN 1: 260)

110.A few days before his passing away, the Swami said:

"I am making ready for death. A great Tapasyâ and meditation has come upon me, and I am making ready for death." (CWSN 1: 261-62)

111.In Kashmir after an illness, Swami Vivekananda said as he lifted a couple of pebbles:

"Whenever death approaches me, all weakness vanishes. I have neither fear, nor doubt, nor thought of the external. I simply busy myself making ready to die. I am as hard as that [the pebbles struck one another in his hand] — for I have touched the feet of God!" (CWSN 1: 262)

www.ingramcontent.com/pod-product-compliance
Lightning Source LLC
Chambersburg PA
CBHW050025170726
48282CB00025B/556
* 9 7 8 9 3 6 8 4 9 0 9 7 5 *